My Friend Has DYSLEXIA

by Amanda Doering Tourville   illustrated by Kristin Sorra

Thanks to our advisers for their expertise, research, and advice:

Anjanette Johnson, M.Ed.
Integrative Medicine Clinic
Children's Hospitals and Clinics of Minnesota

Terry Flaherty, Ph.D., Professor of English
Minnesota State University, Mankato

PICTURE WINDOW BOOKS
a capstone imprint

To Rick, my wonderfully smart and loving husband. Thank you for your help with this book. ADT

Editor: Jill Kalz
Designer: Nathan Gassman
Production Specialist: Jane Klenk
The illustrations in this book were created with mixed media - digital.

Picture Window Books
151 Good Counsel Drive
P.O. Box 669
Mankato, MN 56002-0669
877-845-8392
www.picturewindowbooks.com

Printed in the United States of America in North Mankato, Minnesota.
072010
5843VMI

Library of Congress Cataloging-in-Publication Data
Tourville, Amanda Doering, 1980–
My friend has dyslexia / by Amanda Doering Tourville ; illustrated by Kristin Sorra.
p. cm. — (Friends with disabilities)
Includes index.
ISBN 978-1-4048-5752-0 (library binding)
ISBN 978-1-4048-6111-4 (paperback)
1. Dyslexia—Juvenile literature. 2. Reading disability—Juvenile literature.
I. Sorra, Kristin, ill. II. Title.
LB1050.5.T66 2010
371.91'44—dc22   2009035266

Anna and I have been neighbors and friends since we were little. Anna has a hard time reading. Her doctor says she has dyslexia.

Anna reads out loud slowly. She tries really hard. But sometimes she gets words wrong.

SIGN UP!

ATTENTION
all
students:

pro jects duo
Fribay March12

Science Fair

projects due
Friday, March 12

DID YOU KNOW? Kids with dyslexia can't always make sense of letters and word sounds. They sometimes have trouble reading and spelling. Letters or words may appear switched.

Sometimes kids laugh at Anna when she reads out loud. I tell them to stop. It's not cool to make fun of people.

DID YOU KNOW? Dyslexia is a learning disability. A learning disability is something that makes it hard for a person to process information.

7

Anna needs extra help with her reading.
She goes to special reading classes.

She works
in small groups
or by herself.

DID YOU KNOW? Reading specialists help kids with dyslexia by playing word and spelling games. They also give kids tips for living with dyslexia.

9

Sometimes Anna gets upset with herself. She feels sad because she can't read as easily as the rest of our class. I tell her she's great at lots of other things.

No one can catch a pass like Anna!

DID YOU KNOW? Kids with dyslexia may have low self-esteem. They may feel bad because they have trouble reading.

Anna is amazing at art. She draws pictures of tall buildings and houses. It would be so fun to live in one of them!

DID YOU KNOW? Some famous people have had dyslexia. Scientist Albert Einstein had dyslexia. So did Walt Disney. Actors Tom Cruise, Orlando Bloom, and Keira Knightley all have dyslexia.

13

Anna is a
science whiz.

Science isn't my best subject at all.

Sometimes I help Anna with reading, and she helps me with my science homework.

15

Anna is really good with animals. One day,
Buster ran under the porch and wouldn't come
out. Anna knew just what to do.

Sometimes Anna and **I** just hang out and play video games. We talk about school, sports, and our bossy big brothers.

Anna and I like helping other people.
We started a community club this year.

DID YOU KNOW? Kids with dyslexia may feel left out because they have trouble reading. Doing things for others can help them feel better about themselves.

Our club helps people by collecting food for food shelves.

Anna is awesome! She's kind and caring. I'm lucky to have her as a friend. I try to be a good friend to her, too.

What Is Dyslexia?

Dyslexia is a brain-based learning disability that makes it hard for people to read. It affects people all around the world. People with dyslexia have trouble putting sounds together to make words. They also see letters and words incorrectly. Dyslexia has nothing to do with how smart a person is. Many intelligent people struggle with dyslexia. Tutors and learning specialists help kids with dyslexia by giving them reading and spelling activities. Dyslexia runs in families. If one family member has dyslexia, another member often does, too.

Glossary

learning disability—a condition that keeps a person from learning information the way most people do

process—to make connections between pieces of information

self-esteem—a feeling of being happy with one's self

specialist—a person who knows a lot about a certain thing

tutor—a teacher who gives private lessons

To Learn More

More Books to Read

Edwards, Nicola. *My Friend Has Dyslexia.* North Mankato, Minn.: Chrysalis Education, 2004.

Moore-Mallinos, Jennifer. *It's Called Dyslexia.* Hauppauge, N.Y.: Barron's, 2007.

Robb, Diane Burton. *Alphabet War: A Story About Dyslexia.* Morton Grove, Ill.: Albert Whitman & Co., 2004.

Internet Sites

FactHound offers a safe, fun way to find Internet sites related to this book. All of the sites on FactHound have been researched by our staff.

Here's all you do:

Visit *www.facthound.com*

FactHound will fetch the best sites for you!

Index

Look for all of the books in the Friends with Disabilities series:

My Friend Has ADHD

My Friend Has Autism

My Friend Has Down Syndrome

My Friend Has Dyslexia